A Breeze Swept Through
by
Luci Tapahonso

West End Press
1987

For my brothers

Eugene Tapahonso, Jr.,

Alvin Tapahonso and

Calvin Tapahonso

Poems in this volume have been previously published in the
following magazines and anthologies: *"A" Magazine*, A GATH-
ERING OF SPIRIT, *Ch'iyáán 'iil'ini binaaltsoos* (traditional
cookbook), *Conceptions Southwest*, EARTH POWER COMING,
Maazo Magazine, SONGS FROM THIS EARTH ON TURTLE'S
BACK. Several poems in this volume also appeared in ONE
MORE SHIPROCK NIGHT and SEASONAL WOMAN, earlier
collections by Luci Tapahonso.

This work is partially supported by a grant from the National
Endowment for the Arts, a federal agency.

First printing, October 1987; second printing, May 1989; third
printing, May 1991; fourth printing, June 1994; fifth printing,
September 1997

ISBN 0-931122-45-7

Photo Credit: Armando De Aguero
Cover and Interior Art: Jaune Quick-to-See Smith
Design by: Patt Gateley
Typography by: Prototype

West End Press / P.O. Box 27334 / Albuquerque, NM 87125

TABLE OF CONTENTS

THERE IS NOTHING QUITE LIKE THIS

A Breeze Swept Through

A BREEZE SWEPT THROUGH
For my daughters, Lori Tazbah and Misty Dawn

The first born of dawn woman slid out amid
  crimson fluid streaked with stratus clouds

> her body glistening August sunset pink
> light steam rising from her like rain on warm rocks
> (a sudden cool breeze swept through the kitchen
> and Grandpa smiled then sang quietly,
> knowing the moment).

She came when the desert day cooled and dusk began to move in
in that intricate changing of time   she gasped and it flows

> from her now with every breath with every breath.
> She travels now sharing scarlet sunsets
> named for wild desert flowers
> her smile a blessing song.

And in mid-November, early morning darkness
after days of waiting pain   the second one cried wailing.

> Sucking first earth breath,
> separating the heavy fog,
> she cried and kicked tiny brown limbs.
> Fierce movements as outside
> the mist lifted as the sun is born again.
> (East of Acoma, a sandstone boulder split in
> two — a sharp, clean crack.)

> She is born of damp mist and early sun.
> She is born again   woman of dawn.
> She is born knowing the warm smoothness of rock.
> She is born knowing her own morning strength.

COME INTO THE SHADE

Q: Where are you from?
A: Where I'm from is like this:
                    Hard summer rains
                    leave hollow beads
                    of moisture in the dust.
My mother says each fall:
We have to husk this corn
and throw it on top of the shed
then we'll shell it when it dries.
It's really good in the winter.
                    The dogs raise a racket
                    everytime someone comes home —
                    it's never quiet here.
                    Sometimes the chickens join in
                    then the babies wake up
                    wanting to play.
My father — a thin slightly
bent figure — a shovel over
his shoulder coming home
from the fields. Come into
the shade by the house.
                    The Begays right up on the hill
                    there had a sing last summer.
                    Early in the morning, we went up
                    to watch them dance.
In full view of Shiprock,
there was a drunk man dancing alone,
raising little clouds of dust in the sunlight.
                    We'll just get some mutton
                    at the trading post and cook it
                    under the trees here.
                    Let's make tortillas, too.
                    And pop — regular Pepsi
                    and Diet Pepsi for those on diets
                    (as if it would help after
                    eating ribs!)
Yippee!
Lori said when we sat down to eat.
She knows where she comes from.

I AM SINGING NOW

the moon is a white sliver
balancing the last of its contents
in the final curve of the month

my daughters sleep
in the back of the pickup
breathing small clouds of white in the dark
they lie warm and soft
under layers of clothes and blankets
how they dream, precious ones, of grandma
and the scent of fire
the smell of mutton
they are already home.

i watch the miles dissolve behind us
in the hazy glow of taillights and
the distinct shape of hills and mesas loom above
then recede slowly in the clear winter night.

i sing to myself and
think of my father
teaching me, leaning towards me
listening as i learned
"just like this," he would say
and he would sing those old songs

into the fiber of my hair,
into the pores of my skin,
into the dreams of my children

and i am singing now
for the night
the almost empty moon
and the land swimming beneath cold bright stars.

4

SEASONAL WOMAN
for Marie

I know her
this woman is small, delicate
and doesn't seem to walk like the rest of us.
It's more a gliding movement
she makes to get around.
She soothes her daughters gently
her hair falling down around her face
as she bends down, murmuring comfort
into childhood fears
but don't let that fool you.

I've seen her angry
and she swings up into that pickup cab
in one fast motion
and she drives those rough Shiprock roads
bouncing hard and shifts into
fourth gear fiercely smooth
almost flying-driving
her hair swirling behind
in the hot dust.
That man knows her
and he scurries fast to his mother
when he angers this woman
of fierce seasons and gentle mornings.

THE TREES ALONG THE RIVER

I'll wait until I've circled
the sloping curve of cliffs past Mesita.
The sun is so bright at the top —
shining right in my eyes.
Squinting, I pull the visor down
and look off to the side.
Smooth, red cliffs.

> At the Laguna Tribal Building,
> I said, "I want to see the Governor,"
> and 3 men said, all at once,
> "I'm the Governor,"
> and we all laughed.

The trees along the river
by the trading post have turned a fiery gold
against the gray banks
that are dying for the winter.

> Inside the warm kitchen, she was
> mixing bread dough and she stopped,
> saying, "You know, down at the post
> office, there were some people with
> a case of beer in their pickup and
> someone told the police. The police
> made them pour it all out — they
> didn't even arrest them! We just
> complained about that! The tribal
> police don't do what they should
> these days." Then she said, "Have
> some piñons. There's lots this year."

Coming back, the sun was setting
in my sideview mirror — a square
of brilliant orange hovering at
the corner of my eye — wanting
my attention over and over again.

A DISCREET CONVERSATION

(He was drunk and rolled his car twice
but didn't get hurt.)
           Somehow, he drove his car off the road
           and wrecked his car, his sister said.

General murmurs of sympathy.
           No one knows how it happened,
           his mother added.

Silence.
Then the old grandpa said in a loud voice:
           K'ad ajoodląą láa, ajoolghałiísh
           akojii t'įįh!
           (He was drinking too much, of course,
           that doesn't happen to one
           who has eaten too much!)

Laughter.
           You better go with him
           next time he gets paid!
           They said to his wife.

HILLS BROTHERS COFFEE

My uncle is a small man
in Navajo we call him little father
       my mother's brother.

He doesn't know English but
       his name in the white way is Tom Jim.
       He lives about a mile or so
       down the road from our house.

One morning he sat in the kitchen
drinking coffee
       I just came over, he said,
       the store is where I'm going to.

He tells me about how my mother seems to be gone
everytime he comes over.
       Maybe she sees me coming
       then runs and jumps in her car
       and speeds away!
       He says smiling.
We both laugh just to think of my mother
       jumping in her car and speeding.

I pour him more coffee and
       he spoons in sugar and cream until
       it looks almost like a chocolate shake
       then he sees the coffee can.
       Oh, that's the coffee with
       the man in the dress, like a church man.
       Ah-h, that's the one that does it for me.
       Very good coffee.

I sit down again and he tells me
        some coffee has no kick but
        this one is the one.
        It does it good for me.

I pour us both a cup and
        while we wait for my mother,
        his eyes crinkle with the smile
        and he says
        yes, ah yes, this is the very one
        (putting in more cream and sugar).

So I usually buy Hills Brothers coffee
        once or sometimes twice a day
        I drink a hot coffee and

        it sure does it for me.

DEAR ALVIN

dear alvin,
even now, i fully expect to see you
lying on the living room floor,
watching football and eating pistachios.
as if nothing happened, i bake the cake you like
and take the first bite with your blessing.

    it was like a dream, the day after you died
    we all gathered at home and in mom's warm kitchen,
    we ate and drank coffee.
    we talked: making plans and telling stories
    laughing and remembering all sorts of things:
        your first girlfriend,
        your graduation,
        we even shared some sheep-stealing tales.
    we have good memories and stories.

the clouds were low heavy veils of gray,
we prayed, crying, we buried you,
we returned you to the earth on christmas eve.

the voices   you heard them singing
singing strong and beautiful
they sang navajo hymns
the voices resounding on the flat open spaces
of mesas and clouds, surrounding us, gathering us in
we stood huddled in the wind and cold.
together, we buried you in the strength of ageless songs.

as we drove back to albuquerque, it rained
most of the way — a strong male rain.
at zuni, they say it rains when a good person dies.
it rained. it rained.
as we neared albuquerque, the sun broke through
it was beautiful, rain glistening on the rocks,
rain glistening on the plants, on the roads,
the earth was clean and wet.
the clouds were fluffy — so bright against
the blueness of sky stretching over wet winter earth.

it was there before us: a new strength, a new life.
you have given so much, alvin.
we were grateful for your long-awaited birth:
    "this time it will be a boy,"
    we said to each other hopefully,
    all of us waiting for you.

Ahshénee shishilí,
    nizhónígo shįį diné digyhinii baanenédzá
    nizhónígo shįį nihiba' nanináadoo
    nizhónígo shįį naahiika
    nizhónígo shįį 'áadi kéédahwiit'įįdoo

    we are grateful for your joyous life.
    you have given so much.

NOTE TO A YOUNGER BROTHER

who could help us?
mom and i hung out clothes to dry
crying out loud that morning
i paused and sobbed into her warm shoulder

it was simple enough
   your breath the last two days
   loud and labored
   then slower and slower until the final breath:
      a lasting silence in my memory

   the warm days
   you have known them
   you have seen the shiny shards of broken bottles among rocks
   i am held swaying in the sunlight
   the sunlight thin shell of a teardrop
        cradling me
        i can see through the worn luminescence

one night, months later
i woke crying out loud almost screaming

   i miss you.

      outside the full moon
      watches a large dry leaf
      fall to the ground
          landing with a sigh

it is as you predicted:

    we go on.

A Spring Poem

A SPRING POEM
Song for Misty and Lori

feel good about yourself
>early in the morning
>you can hear the birds chirping, whistling
>right there   right there in the yard
>>listen to them   see how
>>light they are   hopping about

they know the spirits are here
early in the morning before sunrise
in the gray light   the spirits hover about
>go out and welcome them
>savor the morning air
>savor the stillness of little bird noises

they wait for you: the spirits of your grandpa acoma
>the spirits of your uncles
>the spirits of relatives you never knew
>they know you   they marvelled at your birth
>they wait for you saying: come out
>greet us, our little ones
>come out, we want to see you again
they hover waiting in front of the house
by the doors, above the windows
they are waiting to give us their blessing
>waiting to give us their protection

go out and receive them: the good spirits in the gentle-bird morning
they hover singing, dancing in the clean morning air
they are singing   they are singing.

THE LIGHTNING AWOKE US

                    the lightning awoke us
splashing a sudden blue-gray light
                    throughout the room
we lay still
          waiting for the thunder
          it cracked at the mountains
          and rolled westward towards us
          rolling waves of echoes
          a soothing moan above us
then it was quiet outside
          except for the raindrops
          sliding off tree branches
          onto the plastic
          covering the bicycles beneath
          drip   drip   drip   drip
          dropping steadily
i got up then and
          cleared the steam from the window
          expecting to see
          little plastic pools of rain
          hanging between the bicycles
instead the drops slid quickly
          down to the edges of the plastic
          forming bubbles then
          bursting and falling
          into a thin line
          of deep water cracks
          absorbed instantly
          by the dirt   dirt
                    thirsty in the winter.

ALL I WANT

All I want is the bread to turn out like hers just once
        brown crust
        soft, airy insides
        rich and round
that is all.
So I ask her: How many cups?
        Ah yaa ah, she says,
        tossing flour and salt into a large silver bowl.
        I don't measure with cups.
        I just know by my hands,
        just a little like this is right, see?
        You young people always ask
        those kinds of questions,
        she says,
thrusting her arms into the dough
and turning it over and over again.
The table trembles with her movements.
I watch silently and this coffee is good,
                    strong and fresh.
        Outside, her son is chopping wood,
        his body an intense arc.
        The dull rhythm of winter
        is the swinging of the axe
        and the noise of children squeezing in
        with the small sighs of wind
        through the edges of the windows.

She pats and tosses it furiously
shaping balls of warm, soft dough.
        There, we'll let it rise,
        she says, sitting down now.
        We drink coffee and there is nothing
        like the warm smell of bread rising
        on windy, woodchopping afternoons.

YES, IT WAS MY GRANDMOTHER

Yes, it was my grandmother
who trained wild horses for pleasure and pay.
People knew of her, saying:
> She knows how to handle them.
> Horses obey that woman.

She worked,
skirts flying, hair tied securely in the wind and dust.
She rode those animals hard and was thrown,
time and time again.
She worked until they were meek
and wanting to please.
> She came home at dusk,
> tired and dusty,
> smelling of sweat and horses.

She couldn't cook,
my father said smiling,
your grandmother hated to cook.

> Oh Grandmother,
> who freed me from cooking.
> Grandmother, you must have made sure
> I met a man who would not share the kitchen.

> I am small like you and
> do not protect my careless hair
> from wind or rain — it tangles often,
> Grandma, and it is wild and untrained.

FOR LORI, THIS CHRISTMAS
I WANT TO THANK YOU IN THIS WAY

i was nervous, young and so frightened.
you were born late at night (some of my friends were out on dates
that time).

you cried so loudly,
eyes clenched shut,
face pink and already chubby.
i watched stunned by your energy.

oh baby.
you slept soundly all night
and i watched you intently
afraid to sleep (i'd heard all those stories about people who
roll on their babies in their sleep).
i didn't trust myself — conscious or asleep.

early in the morning,
you woke crying —
my heart raced as i reached for you.
i wrapped you tighter in your blanket
and with my finger, i traced the outline of your pulse
just beside the eye (the bone was so tiny and flat,
i thought of kitten bones then).

i circled the pulse,
even slow rhythm then you quieted
   and slept again, tasting your lips and gums.
   you made little lapping sounds.

i was surprised you needed only that:
   gentle touching, quiet little song
   and you gave me a new confidence.
   i had lost it somewhere during that time,
   that easy laughter returned.

i have grown strong since then.
i have grown strong in your laughter.
   i have grown strong in your stories, the pouting and tears.
   i have grown strong in your quick smile and gentle concern.
   i have grown clearer in my thinking.

you told the story at seven to your little brothers and sisters:
   "baby jesus — 'Awééchí'í born somewhere
   on the other side of the world, far, far away
   some sheep, cows and horses saw him and
   they told other sheep, cows and horses.
   and so they know too.
   all of them and all of us know."

This, my daughter, is Christmas.

FOR MISTY STARTING SCHOOL

help her
my shiny-haired child
laboriously tying her shoes
she's a mere child of 4.

she starts school today
smiling shyly
pink heart-shaped earrings
long black hair
      we pause outside the house and pray
      a pinch of pollen for you starting school
      and you, the older sister
      and you, father of bright-eyed daughters.
      with this pollen, we pray
      you will learn easily
      in this new place
      you will laugh and share
      loving people other than us.
      guide her now.   guide us now.
we tell her at school
      sprinkle cornmeal here
      by the door of your classroom.
      she takes some and looks at me
      then lets it fall to the threshold.
              to help my teacher, mommy?
              she asks

yes, to help your teacher
                to help you
                to help us as we leave her now.
oh, be gentle with her
feelings, thoughts and trust.

i tell them again:
remember now, my clear-eyed daughters
remember now, where this pollen
                where this cornmeal is from
                remember now, you are no different
see how it sparkles
feel this silky powder
it leaves a fine trail skyward
as it falls
blessing us
strengthening us.

remember now, you are no different
                blessing us
                leaving us.

Back Then, Sweetheart

BACK THEN, SWEETHEART

he remembers me at 15,
waiting tables in a snug orange dress,
"i liked that," he says smiling.

    and i recall those long desert evenings
    the moon passing swiftly overhead
    when he sang me stories

                stories i wanted to hear
                stories i wanted to live, to live

                we were the stories.

  i watched him then
  carving initials in the picnic table
  because there was no word for us
  no other word for what we were.

  it remains there — the table
  welded to cement in the open spaces near shiprock.
  the initials are barely visible,
  faded by years of cold nights and melting snow.

                yet beneath the surface
                are the songs we sang
                the dance we were, we were.
                that same old moon glides overhead
                countless times again and over again.

back then, sweetheart
anything could happen.
i was already wild with dreams,
lost in dizzy songs of love and forever, ever

     you wanted to hold me,
       hold me steady.

    sweetheart, i spun away.

now it comes to this,
all the years come to this: long afternoon lunches
          we order and taste nothing
          yet we are thirsty, so thirsty
          "a refill, please," i say,
          not looking at the waiter.

these days, pauses in phone conversations
    can mean anything, anything at all.

because beneath warm skin,
      there are private histories,
       desert nights,
       pulsing blood.

LAST YEAR THE PIÑONS WERE PLENTIFUL

it took only a late night phone call
listening and laughing in the bedroom dark
(her husband was lying right there
but one-sided conversations never make sense)

and it made no sense right from the beginning
(the blue moonlight slid down the long center curve of his back
as he got up to take a drink of water)

after the phone call,
she had snow-laced dreams
where she was trying to catch the dark horse
and the other watched, chuckling under his breath
she smelled chamisa when she woke and knew what had happened
     far away the other was going to feed the horses
     beneath toadlena mountains
     the air was heavy with rainscent
     sage and rabbitbrush
but here the morning light bolted into the room in streaks
where her nightgown was a rumpled heap under the bed
and she remembered only the phone call

and the time she followed him into the trading post,
a skinny dog at her heels. He bought her a coke
and they sat on the dusty steps outside, not even talking.
the sun was hot and sticky, fine dirt settling on them.
that was when he said
     it's better here in the spring
     maybe you'll come back then.
as she drove off, she saw him in the rear-view mirror
mounting the dark horse.   that was how it was that day.

here she cleaned the house thoroughly
and at noon he called again saying
                    come on out
                    the clouds are still real low in the mornings
                    but it warms up.
                    we can ride over the mountain if you want.
                    and she did
i have no choice, she told herself
leaving her nightgown on the floor
and her husband waiting at lunch
                    she took the next trailways to gallup,
                    a radio and a can of coffee.

          people saw them at the trading post at newcomb
          reading the bulletin board.
          they left on the dark horse towards two grey hills
          late in the afternoon
                    and weren't seen again that spring.

it doesn't make sense, her husband said,
she seemed happy.
but happiness had nothing to do with it
          and years from now
          her grandchildren will understand, saying
                    back then, those things
                    always happened.

                    that was last year, the piñons were large
                    and the winter — so cold, so cold

                    beneath toadlena mountain,
                    the white desert
                              shining with snow.

SHEEPHERDER BLUES
for Betty Holyan

"Went to NCC for a year,"
she said,
"was alright.
There was some drinking, fights.
I just kept low.
It was alright."

This friend
haven't seen for a year or two.
It was a good surprise.
Took her downtown
to catch the next bus
to Gallup.

"I went to Oklahoma City,"
she said,
"to vacation, visit friends,
have a good time.
But I got the sheepherder blues
in Oklahoma City."

"I kept worrying about my sheep
if they were okay
really missed them,
the long days in the sun.
So after 4 days
I had to leave Oklahoma City."

So she went back,
first bus to Gallup,
then a 2-hour drive
to her sheep.

WILLIE AND ME

these are the times i'm just content
with willie nelson and a can of beer.
      his albums, i mean, she said smiling.

just turn down the lights as you go
and i'll flow even into his hard, sure voice
      until the background drums become
      the rhythm of my pulse.
      ah yes.
      we glide easily around
      this early morning room — willie and me
      and the music is a low moaning
      in this empty space and i know
      that quiver in his voice
      is almost a cry.
      so just leave me here
      in willie nelson sounds
      and the light echo of
      this almost-empty beer can
      against the coffee table

is what she told me then.

YÁADÍ LÁ

he told her
> look. i won't do it no more. honest.
> no more drinking after work. honey.
> t'áá aaníí ádíshní. please.

diníísh łeh. (that's what you always say)
she said over her shoulder.   go on, get out.
go to ruthie.   see if i care.
> so after begging a long time, he finally did go —
> papersacks of clothes, workboots and grimy overalls.

the kids watched quietly until he got into the pickup
then baby said   bye daddy, daddy go bye-bye.
his five-year-old son said   jó t'áá ni ínít'i. shimá doobił yée da.
> (you've brought this upon yourself.
> my mother's not sad.)

he just started the pickup and left — not even waving.
she fed the kids fried potatoes and spam and they watched TV.
later her sister came over, she said,   he's gone, huh?
> mạ'ii' ałt'ạạ dishịị   honey, i won't do it again   'aach' ééh
> noo dah diil whod.   (old coyote was probably saying
> in vain: honey, i won't do it again.)
they just laughed and drank diet pepsi at the kitchen table.

the next night at the powwow,   they saw ruthie
> bik'i dadiítł ịịł, ya'?   (let's really pile it
> on her, shall we?) they asked each other.

nodding, they went to the bathroom and waited
in the stalls.   someone else brought her in and they jumped
her: pulling hair and kicking
            falling all over in loud thumps and grunts
            finally ruthie ran out a little scary-looking,
                        bleeding some.
they brushed themselves off and went out just in time
for the women's fancy shawl number.
        her sister placed first that night.
        it helps to have some excitement
        beforehand, they said laughing.

he came home the next evening and handed her his paycheck
signed.   the kids brought in his sacks of clothes and sat
back down to watch the flintstones.   he sat at the table
and said   i deserve everything you do to me.
            you're just too good for me.
she kept on washing dishes then she asked: ruthie's
            nits' áá' yóóyeelwod?   (she has run away from you?)

he sat awhile not saying anything then went out to get
some wood.   she called her sister up saying:
            ma'ii nádzá!   want to go to town tomorrow?
            'ayóo shibééso holǫ́, hey!   (coyote's back
            and I have money to blow now!)

'índa ma'ií nachxǫǫgo tłóódi naghá jiin'.
(they said the coyote walked around outside that night pouting.)

31

JUST BECAUSE OF THOSE BOOTS

Just because I put on
my deep turquoise blouse and new dark jeans,
he asked, "Are you going to Indian Day at the fair?"

"I don't know," I said,
putting on silver earrings
and strands of coral and turquoise beads,
"it depends on the girls," I said.

He was waiting to see if I was going to put on my boots.

That's a sure sign so I didn't put them on.
Old Indian trick, I thought, slipping on flat brown shoes.

Sometimes no one can be certain of me.

THEY ARE TOGETHER NOW

they were returning from gallup late at night
singing with the radio and laughing
he was driving too fast   too fast
      he missed the curve
          the crash   the immediate silence
they whimpered as
the warm blood spread into the cold asphalt cracks
amidst the glass and tangled metal   their bodies writhed
moaning and crying until they rose above
      they left then   watching in silence

      oh   the soothing silence
         the incredible serenity

they rose   leaving the steaming blood
ticking of metal settling down
the tinkle of glass slipping
the tin whine of a dying radio

         they gather with others now
         in the thin darkness
         airy, light ghosts sometimes they talk laughing
         standing in little groups
         waiting to befriend anyone
         who might happen along

they are happy
on the flat plateau of that other world: death

         that quiet pleasure
         they are all together now.

IT WAS THAT ONE

it was that one from san ildefonso
who kept driving down to albuquerque on warm spring nights
to take me out to dinner or out to dark quiet bars

> where we sat hunched over talking in low voices
> i remember watching the wet drops
> slide down the outside of the tall gin and tonic
> when he said   i have to get home by 11.
> > we're usually through practicing by then.
> (i guess musicians have to keep a tight schedule.)
> > practice is important, he said,
> > waving to the waitress for more salsa.

his wife didn't know anything
but she had asked why there were lots of bugs on the windshield
the last time and when he left at nine or so, i said
> keep in touch by phone, okay?

he smiled   his face a shadow in the empty parking lot
> his car was humming evenly beneath him
> waiting to catch countless insects on
> the dark curving roads back and she would find them
> in the morning   some green streaks mixed with wings
> some hardened red dots and he would have to scrape and scrape
> gritting his teeth without even knowing it
> leaving delicate scratches on the front windshield
> she wanted spotless and clear.

WHO WERE YOU?

who were you that night
after all the beer you drank that long winter day
        who were you?
        angry at nothing and everyone

you drove too fast for the winding canal road
      swerving to the very edge
      where darkened weeds shivered in your rage

i followed you
        my pleading a hardened ache
        you took the night in shreds
            white clouds of breath hung in between screams
            the terror in a sudden billow of dust
                not into the ditch   no
            but the pickup spun and stopped crosswise
            on the road   fading yellow light spilling out
            dust and brakes causing dogs
                to bark with a hoarse urgency

frozen mud glistening
      crumbling as you stumbled
      through cold, stinging bushes
      and how did you fall
         did you slip on a transparent beer bottle?
         (they catch the sharp light of the moon
         and at a certain angle, even the stars)
        or did you slip on a rock
        flat and round
        slick with winter frost?

who were you that night?
who were you that night dying in angry drunkenness?

        hard, winter stars
        motionless in
        the crisp dark night
        the moon, the white moon

THE TIME YOU WILL BE AWAY

I am writing this for you
    the sun is nice
    a warm slant in my office this late winter morning

I am writing this for you
    against the anticipation
    of your leaving two days from now

    it's almost Christmas and you'll be driving
    those flat even roads to Oklahoma   away from me

    the nights will be cold and clear
    as it was last evening when we drove from Gallup after midnight
    (the stars were bright and so, so many)

I am writing this for you and the way the dim moonlight shadows your face
    barely lit by dashboard light
    and lights thrown off by passing trucks

I am writing this for you and the moonlight we share,
    (this car glides quietly over the shiny highway
    and there is no one else on the road)

I am writing this for you and your face as you slept
    the tiny waves in your hair are the way you laugh
    teasing with love and innate stories the way
    your Cherokee grandparents must have done

I am writing this for you and your lips curved like
    the long soothing nights.   Tell me stories and never stop.
    I know how it feels.

I left your house at dawn and drove the long, winding roads home
as the sun rose and mist hovered above the thin river
I left your house with your touch tingling
on my back, hair and arms and
these mornings will hold me until you return.

I am writing this for you and the mornings we share,
(the crows above the river swoop elegantly
and their black feathers glisten like good silver)

I am writing this for you and the fresh cold winter air,
(you'll return with steady prairie winds in your laugh
and Oklahoma winter in your hair)

I will miss you and the night, moon and stars you are.

RAISIN EYES

I saw my friend Ella
with a tall cowboy at the store
the other day in Shiprock.

Later, I asked her
Who's that guy anyway?

Oh Luci, she said (I knew what was coming).
It's terrible.   He lives with me.
And my money and my car.
But just for a while.
He's in AIRCA and rodeos a lot.
And I still work.

This rodeo business is getting to me
you know and I'm going to leave him
because I think all this I'm doing now
will pay off better somewhere else
but I just stay with him and it's hard
because

he just smiles that way you know
and then I end up paying entry fees
and putting shiny Tony Lamas on lay-away again.
It's not hard.

But he doesn't know when
I'll leave him and I'll drive across the flat desert
from Red Rock in blue morning light
straight to Shiprock so easily.

And anyway
my car is already used to humming
a mourning song with Gary Stewart
complaining again of aching and breaking
down-and-out love affairs.

Damn.
These Navajo cowboys with raisin eyes
and pointed boots are just bad news
but it's so hard to remember that
all the time.

She said with a little laugh.

WHOSE LIFE IS THIS?

whose life is this?
whose life is this?

the one who stole
played interstate romance on I-40
       (on summer nights, it's easy, she said later)

she was caught on the trail
of a lone navajo bachelor in a low 280-ZX
       on that undulating stretch from gallup to albuquerque

the one who stole
could say it was those hills, those sheer red cliffs
       that heavy full moon or the night brimming with wildflower scent
      all those elements conspired, she said,
       causing the chase down I-40, it wasn't really me, she said.

the one who stole
sighed and said out loud
          oh no, it's dangerous
       to the empty moonlight car and george strait urging her on

it wasn't really me, she said to herself over and over again
as her husband watched TV at home and her son put together a puzzle
       (a thousand pieces, mom, he said on the phone)

it was the life she stole
that shared the breathing summer horizon
that night with the lone navajo in the fast blue car

later on
the one who stole
was haunted by the freeway hum, summer night breezes
and slow pleading music
          until she gave it back
          the life she stole
          she stole and gave it back
          because it was, she said, a long story
                    like 100 miles long is how she said it

the one who stole will never know
how these things turn out

          these old stories.

IN CERTAINTY, I MOVED TO YOU

I was lying against the warm length of your back
and I dreamed
    we were going through an intersection
    when the car ahead stalled suddenly.
    I swerved around it but
    still metal scraped the back of the car

    as I got out,
    our daughters watched, peering through the back windows,
    faces solemn with fright.

I woke then
in certainty, I moved to you
you gathered me in beneath cool sheets
and we slept again.

It did not suprise me then to find the stereo gone,
    a gaping hole in the dashboard
    the open window waving in the morning air.
    And I swam back into the night,
                the dream,
                that old feeling.

I should have known.

I have only your warm self for certain.

There Is Nothing
Quite Like This

A SONG IN FOUR PARTS

I

that handsome man with gray-blue eyes
would drive 100 miles to have lunch with me
he would, smiling like that.

> he distracts me,
> nowadays i struggle to complete projects
> (i used to be so diligent!)

> be serious, i tell myself, focus on work
> my mind rebels and flies across town
> to where he sits at his desk
> smiling and talking into the phone

II

i should not have spoken to you today
perhaps a smile or a simple "hi" would have sufficed
not that nonsensical rambling i lapsed into

i saw that look of pain and confusion in your eyes
i do that quite well by now

> by now, i have had
> some instances of practice,
> nervous training — putting people on edge
> occurs quite naturally by now.

i won't speak to you when i am this way.

III
i almost danced even closer against you
as we danced around that far corner

just in time, i didn't
instead i looked out at faces alongside the dance floor

>   away from your eyes
>   i didn't want to see what you might have thought
>
>   had i moved   oh so slowly
>   into the empty curve of your arm.

IV
i have been there
oh yes   these nights

>   the breathing land
>   draws us in
>   the full moon reaches out
>   precisely for you
>   precisely for me
>   these shiny highways become trails for where
>   we would go if i wanted, i want
>   we would pass curving hills,
>   pass horses grazing in the moonlight
>   i would leave with you now if you asked.

it is on these nights
i am not sure of my own life   my life becomes a magnet
                                             for what i can't understand.

THEY THINK HE'S SIOUX

on lummi island
there's a tall navajo
who coaches basketball
and cuts timber
they think he's sioux
but i knew
when he said
jóó nizhóníyeí
at the coffee pot.

his eyes are dark
and he smiles slowly
saying
it doesn't snow here.
i might go home to piñon sometime soon.

i knew about
that going home business
because here on the coast
the air is heavy and smells of fish
it's not cold like i thought
quiet heavy days with no sun, no sun
the tall dark pines overhead
drip endless rain
onto the lush undergrowth
of the mountain coast.

THIS IS NICE

this is nice
like this: 2:16 early july morning
outside the full moon
cats walk confidently across the light pools
cast by the street lamps
the dogs are relaxing behind chainlink fences
their ears twitching now and then

my daughters sleep
one watched over by care bears
the other: stereo murmuring in her dreams
they sleep quietly while crickets and kittens
tease each other in the dark corners of the house.

this is nice
to write so much that
sleep is an imposition
to write on nights like this
the moon, the shadows, night sounds,
low music, alive poems and

he loves me,
just like this.

FEAST DAYS AND SHEEP THRILLS

1.
Most feast days are the same:
                    hot sun, good food and lots of cool people.
At Acomita feast, Lori wears her sunglasses
that she's certain make her look 21.

These people are cool.
These people at Acomita feast,
strolling along in mirror sunglasses and cut-off tee-shirts.
They check out everybody else
and lounge on car hoods
putting away fiesta burgers and Shasta pop.

When it starts to rain
they still wear shades even when
the clouds are heavy and thick overhead.

Then rain pours and suddenly it's wrong
to wear a white blouse to a feast.
Women rush to their cars,
arms across their chests.
The cool ones walk as casually as possible
towards their cars.
Once out of sight of other cool ones
they break into a mad run,
ducking their heads and
squinting in the fierce rain.
Finally they carry their shades
in their clenched hands.

2.
People start to leave driving slowly and carefully.
They pause at the small paved sections of the roads to their homes.
The cool ones slouch in the back seats.
The roads home are wide flat ditches of brown rushing waters.

They stop there and wonder what to do.
They say, "They sure must have danced good today."

The feast is over.
The rain is fierce, rushing in torrents across the flat land.
The cool ones are tired and damp.

3.
At the Acomita feast, some booths have signs
that say, "Fresh Hatch green chili"
              underneath underlined in red,
              "REALLY HOT CHILI!!"
Around here, they say, "What's the use if it's not really hot?"

They like their chili mean, you know,
the kind that makes your ears ring, and makes you sweat
and blow your nose.
Of course, they're polite,
leaving the table to do that sort of thing.

Myself, I don't eat it straight.
It's better mixed with beans or the kids' stew,
which is plain without chili.
They tease me about it but it's okay.

I'm Navajo: fry bread and mutton are my specialty.
Like my brother said I get along on sheep thrills.

Some Pueblos just don't understand.

THERE IS NOTHING QUITE LIKE THIS

a cream-colored horse
galloping in the sunrise

circling to the east
        four times
        in the pink morning sky
        look, the streaks of purple
            in gray clouds

the horse runs hard, raising dust
        the dawn is still
        we watch
        there is nothing quite like this to see

the rider: straw hat and rawhide whip
        he yells out on the west side
        of the hooghan
        he yells out four times on the west
            hey!   hey!   hey!   hey!

they have heard
the spirits are coming
they are coming now

the western sky
        a matrix of quick lightning streaks
        in dark, dark clouds

        the lukachukai mountains are damp
        dripping with rain
        even from here in the desert, we know.

we watch
>
>the cream-colored horse and
>the rider with the strong morning yell

take heed,
>
>they circle four times
>around the hooghan
>they have come
>the spirits singing and healing

we are better now for seeing this
>
>a cream-colored horse galloping in circles

the pink sunrise in the warm desert morning

already at 6 am, it's hot and we return
>
>to the fires to cook and
>catch up on the latest stories around this area.